BIGGEST NAMES IN MUSIC

# BILLIE EILISH

by Martha London

FOCUS READERS
NAVIGATOR

## WWW.FOCUSREADERS.COM



Focus Readers is distributed by North Star Editions:
sales@northstareditions.com | 888-417-0195

Produced for Focus Readers by Red Line Editorial.

Photographs ©: Chris Pizzello/Invision/AP Images, cover, 1, 4–5, 7, 24; Shutterstock Images, 8–9, 11, 12, 16, 18, 20–21, 23, 27, 29; Matt Sayles/Invision/AP Images, 14–15

**Library of Congress Cataloging-in-Publication Data**
Names: London, Martha, author.
Title: Billie Eilish / by Martha London.
Description: Lake Elmo, MN : Focus Readers, 2021. | Series: Biggest names in music | Includes index. | Audience: Grades 4-6
Identifiers: LCCN 2020008556 (print) | LCCN 2020008557 (ebook) | ISBN 9781644936337 (hardcover) | ISBN 9781644936429 (paperback) | ISBN 9781644936603 (pdf) | ISBN 9781644936511 (ebook)
Subjects: LCSH: Eilish, Billie, 2001---Juvenile literature. | Singers--United States--Biography--Juvenile literature.
Classification: LCC ML3930.E35 L66 2021 (print) | LCC ML3930.E35 (ebook) | DDC 782.42164092 [B]--dc23
LC record available at https://lccn.loc.gov/2020008556
LC ebook record available at https://lccn.loc.gov/2020008557

Printed in the United States of America
Mankato, MN
082020

## ABOUT THE AUTHOR

Martha London writes books for young readers full-time. She enjoys all types of music. In high school and college, she spent several years performing in musicals.

# TABLE OF CONTENTS

MUSIC ON

## CHAPTER 1

# THE AMERICAN MUSIC AWARDS

Small flames glowed at the back of the stage. The lights were low. Piano music began to play. As the lights came up, Billie Eilish stood in the middle of the stage. She was performing at the 2019 American Music Awards (AMAs). It was her first-ever awards show performance. The teenager had six award **nominations**.

Billie Eilish performs one of her hit songs at the AMAs in November 2019.

Billie began to sing her song "All the Good Girls Go to Hell." Her soft voice rose above the piano. Soon, the music got louder. The energy was building. When it was time for the **refrain**, flames erupted behind Billie. She danced across the stage. People in the crowd jumped up and down. They cheered and sang along with Billie.

Later in the night, Billie was honored with her first award. She won New Artist of the Year. She also took home the award for Favorite Alternative Rock Artist.

Billie was only 17 years old at the time. She was one of the youngest winners in the history of the AMAs. The music world

Billie accepts the award for New Artist of the Year at the 2019 AMAs.

had not seen someone quite like Billie Eilish before. She was known for creating music that doesn't fit into one category. Her performance was a sign that she was going to do amazing things.

BILLIE

CHAPTER 2

# LEARNING BY EXPERIENCE

Billie Eilish Pirate Baird O'Connell was born on December 18, 2001. She grew up in Los Angeles, California. Her brother, Finneas, is four years older. She and Finneas were homeschooled. Billie's parents had worked as actors for years. But when they had children, they took fewer roles. Soon, they stopped acting.

**Billie's brother Finneas plays in her band.**

Billie's parents took on other jobs to pay the bills.

When they were kids, Billie and Finneas were surrounded by music. Their parents encouraged them to make music. Finneas taught himself to play the drums and the

## WHAT'S IN A NAME?

Billie's full name might be long, but each part has a story. *Billie* was the first name of her grandfather. He passed away shortly before she was born. *Eilish* is the Irish form of Elizabeth. Her parents heard the name in a film and loved it. Billie's brother wanted to call her *Pirate*. So that name stuck, too. *Baird* was Billie's mom's last name before she got married. And *O'Connell* comes from Billie's father's side. Billie is proud of her long name.

Finneas has released many songs as a solo artist. He is also an actor, songwriter, and producer.

piano. Billie sang and played the ukulele. Billie was a shy child. She loved to sing. But she hated singing in front of people. Her parents never made her perform if she didn't want to.

Billie plays the ukulele during a performance in the Netherlands.

When Billie was eight years old, she joined the Los Angeles Children's Chorus. It was a big honor. Kids have to **audition** for the group. Not every child is accepted into the choir.

Even though Billie loved music, she had other hobbies. For example, Billie loved horses. When she was growing up, she rode at a barn near her house. Billie's parents could not afford to pay for riding lessons. But that did not stop Billie. She worked at the barn. She cleaned stalls and brushed horses. In exchange, she received lessons.

Billie also danced when she was growing up. She took several different classes. At these classes, she learned different styles of dance. However, when Billie was 14, she injured herself at one of her rehearsals. She had to stop dancing and taking lessons.

CHAPTER 3

# A FAMILY AFFAIR

Billie and Finneas share a close bond. They started making music together when they were kids. Finneas had a band in high school. He wrote a song called "Ocean Eyes" for his band. But he thought the song would sound better if Billie sang it. So, he and Billie recorded the song at home.

**Billie and Finneas accept the award for Record of the Year at the 62nd Grammy Awards.**

Billie performs in Barcelona, Spain, during her world tour in 2019.

When they finished recording the song, Billie and Finneas uploaded it to SoundCloud. SoundCloud is an online music-sharing service. People can listen to songs from artists who do not have recording **contracts**.

Billie and Finneas did not expect the song to be a hit. It was just a fun project for them. But “Ocean Eyes” went viral overnight. It was soon downloaded 10,000 times. The song even got the attention of a record **producer**. When he heard it, he contacted Finneas and Billie. He offered to help them build on their success. In 2016, Billie signed her first recording contract with Interscope Records. She was just 14 years old.

Billie began working on an album. She also began touring. At first, Billie played smaller shows. Her parents bought a van.

Billie's popularity means she has fans all over the world.

They loaded it with equipment. Her dad learned how to run lights for her shows. The whole family traveled together.

In 2019, Billie released her first full-length album. *When We All Fall*

*Asleep, Where Do We Go?* received positive reviews. Billie announced she was going on a longer tour. She performed at larger **venues**. With the new tour, one thing stayed the same. Her family continued to travel with her.

## WRITING SONGS TOGETHER

Many popular singers do not write their own music. They work with songwriters. Billie's **manager** wanted her to work with famous writers on her first album. But Billie did not get along with the writers. She wanted to work with her brother. She and Finneas had a good system. And Billie felt their songs were truer to who she was. Finneas and Billie worked hard together. They co-wrote 11 of the 13 songs on the album. Finneas wrote the other two.

Most of Eilish's first album was recorded in her brother's childhood bedroom.

CHAPTER 4

# JUST GETTING STARTED

It did not take long for Eilish to gain fame. One reason for this is Eilish's unique musical style. She weaves many types of music together. Some songs have a heavy bass that thumps underneath electronic music. Other songs use instruments such as piano and guitar.

Eilish's music is also known for exploring important issues of mental health.

Shortly after releasing her **debut** album, Eilish announced her world tour. She made the announcement at Coachella. This popular music festival takes place in California. Many different musicians come to perform. During

## MENTAL HEALTH

Eilish struggles with **depression**. Her anxiety and depression got worse when she was touring. Eilish does not like being away from her friends for so many months. So, she finds ways to manage. She talks to a therapist. Her friends also fly to visit her when she is touring.

Eilish has had to adjust to her rapidly increasing popularity and the lack of privacy that comes with it.

her tour, Eilish played at another music festival. The Glastonbury Festival is held in England. It is one of the largest music festivals in the world. Eilish's tour continued through 2020.

As producer and songwriter, Finneas joined Eilish in taking home several Grammy Awards in January 2020.

Eilish's first album received a lot of praise. As a result, Eilish was nominated for several awards in 2019, including six Grammy Awards. Eilish was the youngest musician ever to be nominated for all four major categories at the Grammys. They included Best New Artist, Record of the Year, Song of the Year, and Album of the Year. At the awards ceremony, Eilish won all four. She also walked away with the award for Best Pop Vocal Album.

Eilish's music is not the only thing that sets her apart. She is also known for wearing baggy clothes. Eilish chooses to wear this style of clothing because she doesn't want people staring at her body. She doesn't want people judging how she looks.

Some people praised Eilish for covering up. Many other young female artists wear revealing outfits at their concerts.

But Eilish doesn't feel like she is a better person because she wears loose clothes. She thinks people should wear clothes that make them feel comfortable. Eilish wants people to be true to themselves.

Eilish knows that her fame gives her the power to help people. So, she supports causes that are important to her. In 2019, lawmakers in Georgia passed a health-care law that she believed hurt some people, especially women. Eilish had a few concerts coming up in Georgia. She chose to donate some of her concert profits to Planned Parenthood. This organization supports women on a variety of important health issues.

Many people admire Eilish for her unique style, which is very different from the style of other teen pop stars.

Eilish is proud of all her hard work. But she is also humble. She feels lucky for her success. Eilish gets to do what she loves every day.

# BILLIE EILISH

- Birth date: December 18, 2001
- Birthplace: Los Angeles, California
- Family members: Maggie (mother), Patrick (father), Finneas (brother)
- High school: Homeschooled
- Major accomplishments:
    - October 2017: Apple names Eilish its newest Up Next artist.
    - March 2019: *When We All Fall Asleep, Where Do We Go?* is released.
    - August 2019: "Bad Guy" makes it to No. 1 on *Billboard*'s Hot 100 chart.
    - November 2019: Eilish becomes the youngest Grammy nominee ever to be nominated for all four major categories.
    - January 2020: Eilish wins all four major categories at the 62nd Grammys.

Rather than let other people take charge of her clothing, music, and social media, Eilish controls her own image.

- Quote: "I don't even call them fans. I don't like that. They're literally just a part of my life; they're a part of my family. I don't think of them as on a lower level than me. I don't think I'm anything but equal to all of them."

Meghan McKenna. "Billie Eilish Is Wise Beyond Her Sixteen Years." *Fashion*. St. Joseph Media, 19 Apr. 2018. Web. 25 Feb. 2020.

## FOCUS ON
# BILLIE EILISH

*Write your answers on a separate piece of paper.*

1. Write a paragraph summarizing the main ideas of Chapter 3.

2. Do you think people were right to praise Eilish for wearing baggy clothes? Why or why not?

3. How many Grammy Award nominations did Eilish receive in 2019?

   **A.** 4
   **B.** 6
   **C.** 11

4. How might Eilish's music be different if she had worked with more songwriters?

   **A.** It might be too loud.
   **B.** It might not reflect her style as much.
   **C.** It would be the exact same.

*Answer key on page 32.*

# GLOSSARY

**audition**

To try out for a part in a play or musical group.

**contracts**

Agreements that musicians make to work with specific recording companies.

**debut**

The first of something.

**depression**

A medical condition of deep, long-lasting sadness or loss of interest.

**manager**

A person who works with a musician to schedule tour dates and other events.

**nominations**

When people, songs, or albums are chosen as finalists for an award or honor.

**producer**

A person who works with musicians to record songs.

**refrain**

A repeated section of a song.

**venues**

Places where performances happen.

# TO LEARN MORE

## BOOKS

Erickson, Marty. *Work in the Music Industry.* San Diego, CA: ReferencePoint Press, 2020.

Klepeis, Alicia. *Music Trivia: What You Never Knew About Rock Stars, Recording Studios, and Smash-Hit Songs.* North Mankato, MN: Capstone Press, 2019.

National Geographic Kids. *Turn It Up! A Pitch-Perfect History of Music That Rocked the World.* Washington, DC: National Geographic Kids, 2019.

## NOTE TO EDUCATORS

Visit **www.focusreaders.com** to find lesson plans, activities, links, and other resources related to this title.

# INDEX



**Answer Key: 1.** Answers will vary; **2.** Answers will vary; **3.** B; **4.** B